YOUR LAND
AND
MY LAND

We Visit
PANAMA

Bonnie

Hinman

Mitchell Lane
PUBLISHERS

P.O. Box 196
Hockessin, Delaware 19707

Visit
PANAMA

Brazil

Chile

Colombia

Cuba

Dominican Republic

Mexico

Panama

Puerto Rico

Peru

Venezuela

YOUR LAND AND MY LAND
We Visit
PANAMA
PORTUGAL
Lisbon
Madrid
SPAIN
Barcelona
Algiers
Rabat
Casablanca
MOROCCO
RIDGE
PENEDOS DE SÃO PEDRO E SÃO PAULO (BRAZIL)
ARQUIPÉLAGO DE FERNANDO DE NORONHA (BRAZIL)
tasco

Copyright © 2011 by Mitchell Lane Publishers, Inc. All rights reserved. No part of this book may be reproduced without written permission from the publisher. Printed and bound in the United States of America.

Printing   1   2   3   4   5   6   7   8   9

Library of Congress Cataloging-in-Publication Data
Hinman, Bonnie.
  We visit Panama / by Bonnie Hinman.
    p. cm. — (Your land and my land)
  Includes bibliographical references and index.
  ISBN 978-1-58415-893-6 (library bound)
  1. Panama—Juvenile literature. I. Title.
  F1563.2.H56 2010
  972.87—dc22
                                                    2010019390

PUBLISHER'S NOTE: This story is based on the author's extensive research, which she believes to be accurate. Documentation of this research is on page 61.

The Internet sites referenced herein were active as of the publication date. Due to the fleeting nature of some web sites, we cannot guarantee they will all be active when you are reading this book.

To reflect current usage, we have chosen to use the secular era designations BCE ("before the common era") and CE ("of the common era") instead of the traditional designations BC ("before Christ") and AD (*anno Domini,* "in the year of the Lord").

Contents

Introduction

Latin America is known for vibrant mixtures of cultures and cuisines, for tropical paradises and colorful wildlife, and in some places, for violent weather and political turmoil. Latin America is the name given the regions of North, Central, and South America where languages based on Latin are spoken. Those languages include Spanish, Portuguese, and some variations of French. People in the United States commonly think of all nations south of the U.S. borders as being part of Latin America. It includes Mexico, many of the Caribbean Islands, and the countries in Central America and South America. The country of Panama is in the narrowest part of Central America. That geography has determined much of Panama's place in the world.

The Regions and Countries of Latin America

LATIN
AMERICA

Caribbean: Cuba, the Dominican Republic, French
West Indies, Haiti, and Puerto Rico
North America: Mexico
Central America: Belize, Costa Rica, El Salvador,
Guatemala, Honduras, Nicaragua, Panama
South America: Argentina, Bolivia, Brazil, Chile,
Colombia, Ecuador, French Guiana, Guyana,
Paraguay, Peru, Suriname, Uruguay,
Venezuela

The view from Ancon Hill in Panama City includes Punta Paitilla, an exclusive waterfront neighborhood on a spit of land in downtown Panama City. Ancon Hill was part of the Panama Canal Zone. It has remained undeveloped and is now a protected nature area.

Welcome to Panama

Crossing Panama in Central America is the shortest way to go from the Atlantic Ocean to the Pacific Ocean. The country is an isthmus, a narrow strip of land that joins two larger pieces of land and has water on its long sides. Panama bridges Central and South America. If you wanted to travel by land from the United States to Mexico and then south to Brazil, you'd have to go through Panama.

At one of Panama's narrowest points is its most famous attraction—the Panama Canal. The canal was finished in 1914 after almost 10 years of construction by the United States. Before that the French had tried to build a canal across Panama but failed. The Panama Canal is 50 miles (80 kilometers) long, and it takes a large cargo ship 8 to 10 hours to travel from one end to the other.

The canal has locks, which are like steps that take a ship up to the next level of water. Each end of the canal is at sea level, but the land gradually raises inland from each side. When the French started building a canal across the country in 1881, they were building a sea level canal. To make the water flow from one coast to the other would require that a huge ditch be dug through the land. The French would have had to remove millions of tons of rock and soil from a pass through the mountains of the Continental Divide. This mistake in their plans was the main reason for their failure.

Locks are built of cement and look a little like huge swimming pools. Building them was considered one of the biggest engineering feats of the twentieth century. The canal locks have a fairly simple design that allows ships to be raised or lowered to different water levels so that they can step up to higher land in the interior of Panama and step back down to sea level at the other coast.

Panama's destiny has almost always been determined by geography. The narrow stretch of land that separates one ocean from another has given Panama much greater importance in the world than a small Latin American country might expect. Ever since the first Spanish explorers set foot on Panama, the country has played a major role in world

economics. The Spanish used Panama to transport gold from Peru, the forty-niners used it as a shortcut to California for the gold rush, and the United States wanted to keep Panama happy to ensure that cargo ships could move quickly from one U.S. coast to the other.

Panama has a rich mixture of people and cultures today because of its long history of being a crossroads for commerce. The Panamanian people have overcome many obstacles, including great political unrest, to flourish today as a modern country with a bright future.

The massive Gatun Locks are on the Caribbean side of the Panama Canal. The three pairs of lock chambers are each 1,000 by 110 feet (almost 305 by 34 meters). The view from an observation tower shows the different levels of water in the lock chambers, the Caribbean entrance to the locks, and Lake Gatun.

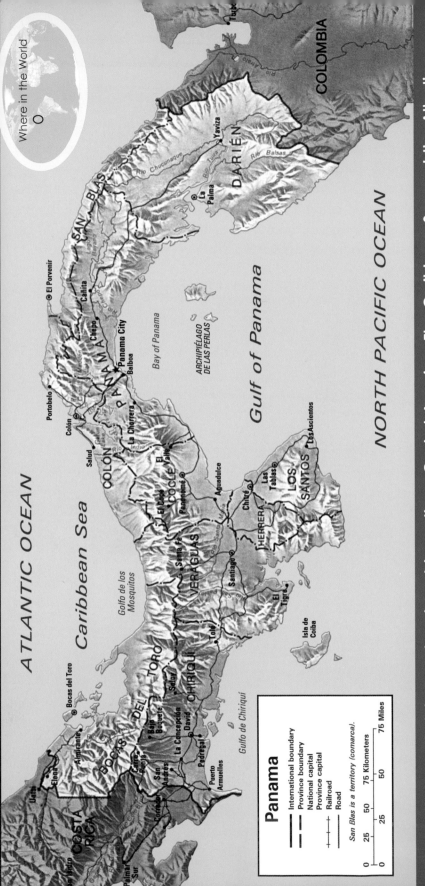

Where in the World ○

ATLANTIC OCEAN

Caribbean Sea

COLOMBIA

DARIÉN

SAN BLAS

Yaviza

Río Balsas

La Palma

El Porvenir

Cañita

Chepas

Panama City

Balboa

Bay of Panama

ARCHIPIÉLAGO DE LAS PERLAS

Gulf of Panama

NORTH PACIFIC OCEAN

Portobelo

Colón

COLÓN

La Chorrera

Salud

El Caño

COCLÉ

El Valle

Penonomé

Aguadulce

LosAscientos

Las Tablas

LOS SANTOS

HERRERA

Chitré

El Tigre

Santiago

VERAGUAS

Santa Fe

Golfo de los Mosquitos

Isla de Coiba

BOCAS DEL TORO

Bocas del Toro

Almirante

Elena

COSTA RICA

Soloy

Bajo Boquete

David

La Concepción

Pedregal

Puerto Armuelles

San Andrés

Cerro Punta

CHIRIQUÍ

Gulfo de Chiriquí

Palmar Sur

Río Claro

Tolé

Panama

— — — International boundary
– – – Province boundary
● National capital
◉ Province capital
+—+—+ Railroad
——— Road

San Blas is a territory (comarcal).

| 0 | 25 | 50 | 75 Kilometers |
| 0 | 25 | 50 | 75 Miles |

Panama stretches east and west in southern Central America. The Caribbean Sea and the Atlantic Ocean lie to the north of Panama, while the Pacific Ocean is south of Panama. For those on the eastern coast of Los Santos province, because the Azuero Peninsula juts into the North Pacific Ocean, the sun rises over the Pacific.

PANAMA FACTS AT A GLANCE

Official name: Republic of Panama

Size: 29,120 square miles (75,420 square kilometers); slightly smaller than South Carolina

Population: 3,360,474 (July 2009 est.)

Capital: Panama City (pop. 1.1 million)

Holy Ghost orchid

Highest point: Volcán Barú (11,398 feet/3,475 meters)

Lowest point: Pacific Ocean—0 feet (0 meters)

Ethnic groups: Mestizo (mixed Amerindian and white) 70%, Amerindian and mixed (West Indian) 14%, white 10%, Amerindian 6%

Religious groups: Roman Catholic 85%, Protestant 15%

Languages: Spanish, English

Climate: Hottest month—April; Coolest month—September

Exports: Bananas, shrimp, sugar, coffee, clothing

Imports: Capital goods, foodstuffs, consumer goods, chemicals

Agricultural products: Bananas, rice, corn, coffee, sugarcane, vegetables; livestock; shrimp

Flag: Panama's flag was officially adopted on June 4, 1904. The white parts stand for peace; the blue star stands for purity and honesty; and the red star stands for law and power.

National flower: Holy Ghost Orchid, or Dove Orchid (*Peristeria elata*)

National bird: Harpy eagle

Source: *CIA World Factbook*, Panama

 The harpy eagle is found in the Darién region. Weighing up to 20 pounds (9 kilograms), it is one of the world's most powerful birds of prey.

Vasco Núñez de Balboa was part explorer and part scoundrel. His rival Pedrarias, the governor of the isthmus in 1518, had Balboa arrested on trumped-up charges of treason. After a show trial, Balboa was beheaded in January 1519.

A Long History

Archaeologists who have excavated ancient villages in Panama estimate that people migrated there as long ago as 2500 BCE. These first known settlers, the Amerindians, include such tribes or groups as the Kuna, Cueva, and Coclé peoples.

The first European known to have seen the coast of Panama was Rodrigo de Bastidas, who sailed along the Caribbean shore in 1501. Christopher Columbus was next as he continued his lifelong search for a water route to the East Indies. He explored the coast in 1502 and met the people who lived there. He noticed that the natives had gold adornments, which caught the attention of his men. Columbus may have wanted to find a way to the Orient, but most Spanish explorers and King Ferdinand of Spain were more interested in finding gold—and lots of it.

In 1513, Vasco Núñez de Balboa made his famous trip across the Isthmus of Panama. As far as is known, Balboa was the first European to view the eastern Pacific. He first saw Panama in 1501 when he was a seaman on Bastidas's ship as it sailed along the coast. After that he spent a few years in Hispaniola, where he got into serious financial trouble. He stowed away on a ship that was traveling to Panama but was discovered. The ship's captain wanted to leave him on a deserted island, but Balboa made himself useful because of his knowledge of the isthmus.

Eventually Balboa was put in charge of Santa María de la Antigua, the first European settlement to survive in Panama. He was a brutal leader, especially to the natives who opposed his rule. The native people told stories about a huge sea to the south, with cities of gold along the coastline. On September 1, 1513, the gold-hungry Balboa set out to investigate the stories.

Balboa took 190 men with him plus a large group of natives. It was a hard journey, and the chiefs of the lands the Spaniards crossed were not happy to see them. The Spaniards fought the local tribes even as more and more of the soldiers succumbed to diseases such as malaria and yellow fever. On September 25, 1513, Balboa climbed over a ridge and saw the waters of the Pacific Ocean in the distance.

Statue of Captain Henry Morgan

Four days later he reached the ocean's edge and waded into the surf dressed in full armor. He claimed the entire sea and all the lands it touched for the Spanish Crown. Only 67 of the 190 men who had traveled with him survived to stand in the waters of what Balboa named the South Sea. In 1520, Ferdinand Magellan renamed it the Pacific.

The original Panama City, now called Panama La Vieja, was founded in 1519 by a Spanish conquistador named Pedro Arias Dávila, known as Pedrarias. The city was built mostly of wood, and in 1671, Welsh pirate Henry Morgan burned it down—along with all its riches. None of the ruined buildings are perfectly preserved, but several stone buildings remain partially intact. The Cathedral Tower and the Casa Del Obispo (Bishop's House) are the best preserved of the ruins.

After the destruction of Panama La Vieja, the Spanish moved Panama City southwest to a location that could be better protected from such pirates as

Originally known as Catedral de Nuestra Señora de la Asunción, the Cathedral Tower is almost all that is left of the first Panama City. The name of the cathedral was transferred to a new cathedral built in Casco Viejo.

Morgan. Called Casco Viejo, it became a city within a city and reflects what most tourists consider to be the real Panama. Narrow brick streets are bordered by Spanish and French colonial-style homes, with wrought-iron balconies filled with tropical plants.

Panama was part of the Spanish Empire for a little over 300 years. The Spanish established towns and trade routes, but colonization was not their primary goal. They wanted to make their fortunes quickly and thought that finding gold was the best way to do so. They built the legendary Camino Real to move gold from Peru and Mexico across Panama to the Caribbean Sea.

The native peoples were used as sources of information about gold deposits and as slaves. Spaniards brought devastating diseases to the

Amerindians, who had no immunities to the European germs. Many of those who survived disease and mistreatment by the Spaniards eventually fled into the forests and to nearby islands.

By the 1820s, freedom fever was sweeping the Spanish New World, as Colombia, Venezuela, and Chile, among others, declared their freedom from Spain. In 1821, Panama also declared independence. The following years were turbulent as Panama joined with Colombia to form Gran Colombia. By this time the United States had seen the value of Panama and began to intervene in disputes in the region.

In 1848 the gold rush to California began in the United States. Gold-seekers arrived in Panama to make a quicker crossing than could be made by boat around Cape Horn in South America or overland across the western plains and mountains of the United States. Those who left in 1849, called forty-niners, were willing to pay well to cross Panama.

American merchant William Henry Aspinwall saw the opportunity to make a fortune, and in 1850 his company began building a railroad across Panama. The railroad was finished in 1855 and charged US$25 in gold—an enormous sum in those days—for a one-way trip to the Pacific. Construction was expensive in both money and lives, as thousands of workers died from accidents and disease.

In the 1880s, France decided to build a canal across Panama. The French sank massive amounts of money and manpower into the effort, but by 1888 the French canal company had run out of money. Much of the machinery they had brought to Panama was left to rust in the humid jungle. An estimated 20,000 to 22,000 people lost their lives while working on this project, most to disease.

Meanwhile, Panama and Colombia feuded off and on, and Panama tried several times to separate from its neighbor. Finally, in 1903, U.S. President Theodore Roosevelt took advantage of another rift between Panama and Colombia to gain control of the land thought to be best suited for building a canal. The United States supported Panama as it declared its independence from Colombia that year. In return, Panama leased a 10-by-50-mile zone to the United States in perpetuity.

The United States was not trying to help a new country gain its freedom. Rather, it was a clear-headed bid to get and keep control of the means for ships to cross from one ocean to another in a fraction of the usual time.

The lock-design canal was begun in 1904 and finished in 1914, under budget and ahead of schedule. Construction was not without problems or expense, but the lessons of the French had been well learned. Housing and dining halls were built for the workers, and major efforts were made to rid the Canal Zone of the deadly diseases that had crippled the railroad workers and the French before them.

In 1897, Ronald Ross discovered that *Anopheles* mosquitoes carried the parasite that causes malaria; and in 1901, Walter Reed discovered that *Aedes aegyypti* mosquitoes carried the virus that causes yellow fever. When this news reached the mosquito-infested Canal Zone, U.S. Army Dr. William Gorgas was appointed to rid the zone of the insects. Gorgas had served in Cuba during and after the Spanish-American War along with Reed. The two doctors had great success in getting rid of mosquitoes in Cuba, so Gorgas knew what to do in Panama when he arrived in 1904.

Gorgas struggled with U.S. authorities, who weren't so sure that mosquitoes were to blame for yellow fever and malaria. He persisted and was finally given the equipment and manpower he needed to mount a fight against the insects. Each day a small army of men walked the streets of Panama City, Colón, and other smaller settlements. They fumigated, screened open windows, and removed standing water. Yellow fever and malaria sufferers were also strictly quarantined, since it had been determined that the mosquitoes must feed on a victim's blood in order to spread the disease.

Gorgas's war on mosquitoes was dramatically successful. By 1906 yellow fever was virtually wiped out in Panama. Malaria was harder to get rid of, but the death rate among Panama Canal employees from malaria dropped from a peak of 7.45 per 1,000 employees in 1906 to 0.30 deaths per 1,000 in 1913.

The canal opened and shipping began on August 15, 1914. The U.S. project claimed more than 5,500 lives, and the cost reached $352 million.

The Panama Canal operated successfully, with few problems. The Canal Zone became like a small U.S. settlement. Panamanians some-

The Gatun Locks had their first trial run on September 26, 1913. The tugboat, *Gatun*, proceeded slowly through the locks, a process that took almost two hours. Soon the locks were used daily to move dredges, barges, and tugs up into Lake Gatun as they cleared the Culebra Cut of landslide debris.

times resented the U.S. presence and felt they had been cheated. Because of this resentment, the treaty was changed several times. The "in perpetuity" wording in the original treaty was dropped; the canal and the Canal Zone would be leased for a certain amount of time with a guaranteed renewal.

After anti-American riots in 1964, U.S. President Lyndon B. Johnson announced that the United States would negotiate yet another canal treaty with Panama. These negotiations continued with slow progress until 1977, when U.S. President Jimmy Carter and Panamanian President Omar Torrijos signed a new treaty that called for the gradual turnover of the canal to Panama.

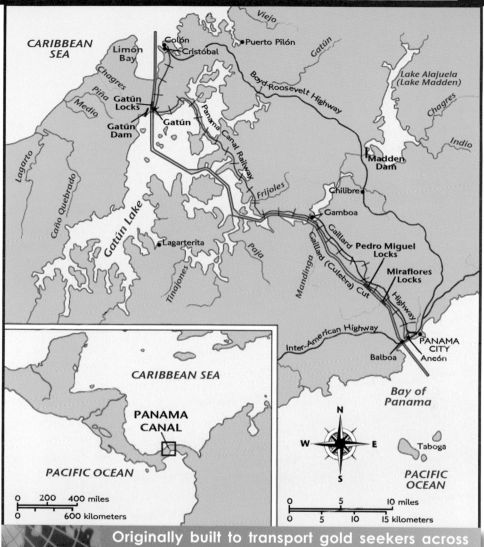

Originally built to transport gold seekers across Panama during the California gold rush, the Panama Railroad ran daily trips during the Canal Zone days. It fell into disrepair during the 1980s and was not put back into service until the late 1990s. Now it mainly serves as a cargo route with one daily passenger trip.

At noon on December 31, 1999, Panama took over the operation of the canal and control of the former Canal Zone. Within a decade, a canal renovation project was under way. It would greatly expand the capacity of the canal, allowing even larger ships to use the waterway.

Panamanian President Ricardo Martinelli and U.S. President Barack Obama attended a reception at the New York City Metropolitan Museum on September 23, 2009. Panama and the United States have always had a close relationship.

Presidents and Dictators

Mireya Moscoso, the first woman president of Panama, was in office during the transfer of the canal to Panama. She was the widow of Arnulfo Arias, who had been president three times but because of political unrest never finished a term. Moscoso met her husband while working on his reelection campaign in 1968. After a military coup, Arias and Moscoso were forced into exile in Florida, where they lived until Arias died in 1988.

After her husband's death, Moscoso returned to Panama and entered politics. She first ran for president in 1994 but came in second in the race. She ran again in 1999 and was elected. Moscoso took office in September 1999, just in time to oversee the Panama Canal transfer. The changeover went smoothly, and was helped by the fact that she allowed the Panama Canal Authority to remain independent of politics.

Panama is a constitutional democracy just like the United States. There is a president and a vice president. They are elected to five-year terms. They may serve more than one term, but the terms cannot be consecutive.

The president lives in the Presidential Palace, which is also called El Palacio de las Garzas, or Palace of the Herons. The palace is located in Casco Viejo and overlooks Panama Bay. It is called the Herons' Palace because in 1922, Panama received a gift of African herons, and flocks of them still roam the palace courtyards.

The legislature is a unicameral (one house) body of 71 members. They serve five-year terms at the same time as the president. Panama has a supreme court, with nine justices who serve ten-year terms, as well as several superior courts and courts of appeal.

Panama has technically been a democracy since it gained independence from Colombia in 1903, but the reality was different for most of the twentieth century. From 1903 until 1968, it was governed under a democratic constitution but was dominated by a commercially oriented oligarchy. (An oligarchy is a form of government in which power rests with a small group of elite families or individuals.)

Since the Spanish arrived, Panama has operated under a strictly observed class system. The original Spaniards and their descendents were at the top and everyone else was at the bottom. This division softened some as foreigners came to Panama to live and intermarried with the Spanish, and as some native Panamanians became more successful. However, the government was still controlled by as few as ten families who had high stakes in Panama's commercial success.

In the 1950s the military began to challenge the way the upper-class oligarchy controlled the country. In 1968 the military ousted the elected president, Arnulfo Arias, and took over running the country. General Omar Torrijos headed the military and became the country's leader. His regime was corrupt and harsh, but he became popular with the previously ignored rural and urban lower classes when he started programs to benefit them. He was also anti-American, which appealed to the Panamanians who, unlike the upper classes, saw no benefits to having the United States operate the Canal Zone. In fact, they resented the Americans.

Torrijos was killed in a plane crash in 1981, and by 1983 the military was

Heron in the palace

controlled by General Manuel Noriega. This general was much different from Torrijos, who had been popular and charismatic. Noriega ruled by fear.

Noriega began his rise to ultimate power in the early 1980s as head of the Panamanian National Guard, which he renamed the Panamanian Defense Forces (PDF). Presidents were still elected by the people, but the candidates who won were chosen by Noriega and elected by means of fraudulent vote counting.

Noriega was not the first dictator to rule Panama, but he would be the worst and probably the last. True democracy has had only a slight hold on Panama since the 1930s when the first military coup took place.

A new election was held in May 1989, and it appeared that opposition candidate Guillermo Endara had won. Noriega nullified the election and installed his candidate as the winner. International election observers, including former U.S. President Jimmy Carter, declared the election a fraud. Ballots had been destroyed, votes bought, and voters turned away from the polls. A few days later a protest march led by Endara was attacked by the PDF. The protesters were beaten and shot at with buckshot and tear gas. Endara was hit on the head with a steel pipe and suffered a concussion.

As Noriega increased his grip on Panama, some of his military associates began to question his erratic behavior. In October 1989,

Manuel Noriega ruled Panama with terror and violence from late 1983 until he was ousted in December 1989.

one of his generals mounted a coup to oust him. The coup was stopped, and its leaders were tortured and executed.

Periodic violent clashes between the PDF and U.S. soldiers who traveled outside the Canal Zone continued. The last straw came on December 16, 1989, when U.S. Marine Robert Paz was stopped at a PDF checkpoint in Panama City. Paz was on leave and had just left a restaurant. The PDF soldiers harassed him until he panicked and tried to flee. The PDF shot him dead. On December 20, President George H.W. Bush ordered Operation Just Cause—an invasion of Panama. The time had come to remove Noriega from power.

Operation Just Cause employed over 27,000 troops and 300 aircraft. By the time the fighting ended in the first week of January, 23 U.S. soldiers had been killed and 325 wounded. The PDF was estimated to have lost around 200 soldiers. Civilians paid the highest price in Operation Just Cause. Casualty estimates vary widely, but they numbered at least several hundred.

Noriega escaped the PDF headquarters to request asylum at the home of the Vatican representative in Panama. After he surrendered on January 3, 1990, he was tried and sentenced to 40 years in prison. That sentence was later reduced, ending in 2007. He remained in custody in Florida, fighting extradition to France. In April 2010, France was finally able to move him to Paris to face money-laundering charges. Meanwhile, Panama asked that he be returned to Panama to face charges there as well, for which he could serve an additional 20 years in prison.

A period of turmoil followed the ousting of Noriega, but Guillermo Endara was declared the elected president and was sworn into office the day the invasion began. He served out his term and was succeeded by Ernesto Pérez Balladares after a fair election in 1994.

The PDF was disbanded, and since then Panama has not maintained a military force. A civilian police force was trained and democracy began to take hold at last.

When Mireya Moscoso served as president, from 1999 until 2004, she was both applauded and condemned for her actions during her term. She established a Truth Commission to investigate the unexplained disappearance of 110 people during the Torrijos and Noriega dictatorships. On the other hand, although Panama's economy was growing when she took office, the global economic downturn hit Panama hard. Moscoso was blamed for this particularly when she gave expensive watches and earrings as Christmas presents to the 71 members of the National Assembly. Her administration was also plagued with accusations of corruption.

The son of former dictator Omar Torrijos, Martín Torrijos, was elected president in 2004. His term was marked by union troubles and a public health crisis when tainted cough syrup killed dozens of people before the government stepped in to investigate. But the economy improved, and so did Torrijos's popularity when he supported the expansion of the Panama Canal. The expansion was approved by a vote of the people in 2006.

Ricardo Martinelli was elected president in May 2009. He inherited a healthy economy whose growth was predicted to be 9.2 percent by 2012. Most important, the Panama Canal renovation was proceeding on schedule and without major problems.

Before Mireya Moscoso became president of Panama, she helped create the Arnulfista political party, which was named after her husband, former President Arnulfo Arias.

Coiba National Park in Panama is a scuba diver's paradise. A total of 760 species of fish, including these king angelfish, and 33 species of sharks have been found there.

Biodiversity Unlimited

Panama is not oriented north and south but rather east to west. Its shape is sometimes confusing to visitors. It is like a letter S turned on its side, with the Caribbean Sea to the north and the Pacific Ocean to the south. A ship traveling from the Pacific side of the Panama Canal to the Caribbean side actually exits the canal west of where it started.

Panama covers 29,120 square miles (75,420 square kilometers), making it slightly smaller than South Carolina. It is at the eastern end of Central America, with Costa Rica on the west and Colombia on the east. The oceans are only 50 miles (80 kilometers) apart at the Panama Canal in the middle of the country, and that isn't the narrowest part of the isthmus.

Panama has several mountain ranges, including the Cordillera Central, which runs east and west in the middle of the country from Costa Rica toward the canal. Another large range runs along the Caribbean coast. Altogether nearly 78 percent of Panama is mountainous. There are also swamps, coastal beaches, tropical rain forests, coral reefs, and hundreds of islands on both sides of the isthmus. The country also has around 500 rivers.

Since Panama lies so close to the equator (between 7 and 10 degrees north of it), days and nights are about the same length year round. The sun rises between 6:00 and 6:30 A.M. and sets between 6:00 and 6:30 P.M. It also gives it a tropical climate, with temperatures that vary little throughout the year. In the lowlands, temperatures range from 90°F (32°C) during the day to 70°F (21°C) at night. The highland

Vegetable fields cling to the steep slopes of mountains near the town of Guadalupe in Chiriqui. Erosion and overuse of pesticides, results of intensive farming, have become serious environmental problems in this picturesque paradise.

temperature range is much wider, and frost may form at the top of Volcán Barú, Panama's highest mountain. Along the coasts, evening breezes from the lowlands make the temperatures more bearable. The humidity is quite high all the time.

Panama has only two seasons. The dry season (summer) lasts from December to April, while the rainy season (winter) lasts through the other seven months or so. In some parts of Panama, the changing of the seasons brings unsettled weather—usually heavy rains. One weather problem Panama doesn't have is hurricanes. Prevailing winds and currents carry hurricanes north of Panama.

Toucan

The seasonal rains in Panama are both a blessing and a curse. Average yearly rainfall there is more than 9 feet (3 meters). The Caribbean side is much wetter than the Pacific side. The rains fill Gatun Lake, which allows the Panama Canal to operate, but they also regularly wash out roads and bridges and cause flooding. The heaviest rains come in October and November, but thunderstorms arrive almost daily during the entire rainy season.

Panama is home to an amazing number of species of plants and animals. So far, 972 species of birds have been identified in Panama, along with more than 200 mammal species and 200 reptile species. Plants weigh in with more than 10,000 species. About 1,500 of Panama's plant species occur nowhere else on earth.

Panama is paradise for orchid lovers, since it can boast more than 1,000 orchid species. In fact, the national flower is the Holy Ghost or Dove orchid. Some of the hundreds of kinds of trees include the Panama tree, which is thought of as the national tree, plus the kapok, the wild cashew, and the strangler fig. The strangler fig is well named: It begins its life on a host tree and gradually strangles it to death.

Bird species include the toucan, which can be seen in the Soberanía National Park, and

Passiflora miniata flower

Quetzal

the national bird of Panama, the harpy eagle, which lives in the dense jungles of La Amistad National Park. The quetzal, often called the most beautiful bird in the world, lives in the cloud forests on the slopes of Volcán Barú, a dormant volcano.

Panama's forests are home to big cats like jaguars and ocelots, as well as many kinds of monkeys, including howler and spider monkeys. Capybaras look like giant guinea pigs. Weighing up to 100 pounds (45 kilograms), they are the world's largest rodents. There are several kinds of deer, as well as giant anteaters, peccaries, sloths, and Baird's tapirs.

Five kinds of sea turtles visit the waters off Panama, and four kinds lay their eggs in its sandy beaches. Manatees, dolphins, and sharks live among brightly colored tropical fish. Frogs and reptiles, including several venomous snakes, abound. The fer-de-lance, a pit viper, is one of the more deadly. The bushmaster is the largest venomous snake in the western hemisphere.

Perhaps the rulers of the species by their force of numbers are the insects. It is hard to even imagine the numbers to be found. There are 10,000 species of beetles alone, and 16,000 kinds of butterflies. There are army ants, giant cockroaches, stinging centipedes, and arachnids, including scorpions, tarantulas, and the golden orb spider.

Panama's biodiversity and abundance of plants and animals draw scientific researchers from throughout the

Sloth

Weighing up to 700 pounds (320 kilograms), the endangered Baird's tapir is the largest land mammal found from Mexico to South America. The animal shares common ancestry with hippos and horses. It has a tough hide and eats plants and leaves.

world. In the Amador section of Panama City, at the Pacific entrance to the Panama Canal, the Bridge of Life Museum of Biodiversity celebrates this variety. It was scheduled to open in 2011.

Beetle (magnified) in Parque Nacional Santa Fé, Verguas, Panama

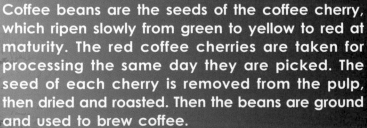

Coffee beans are the seeds of the coffee cherry, which ripen slowly from green to yellow to red at maturity. The red coffee cherries are taken for processing the same day they are picked. The seed of each cherry is removed from the pulp, then dried and roasted. Then the beans are ground and used to brew coffee.

Making a Living

It's easier to find a job in Panama than in many other Latin American countries. Panama's unemployment rate is about 7 percent, although economists classify many workers as underemployed, such as street vendors or those who do sewing at home. These people work but make barely enough money to support their families. Agricultural jobs are abundant but low paying. Unlike most Latin American nations, Panama is not dependent on agriculture as a major source of income.

In the western Panama highlands, east of Volcán Barú, the Boquete area is a prime coffee growing region. Boquete coffee farmers grow some of the best coffee in the world, and they grow it in the shade.

To produce shade-grown coffee, farmers plant the coffee bushes under larger trees. Orange trees are often planted to shade the bushes, and they also offer an additional crop. Farmers say that using this method protects the coffee bushes from pests, produces natural mulch, and requires less fertilizer. The yield is somewhat lower than coffee grown in the open, but farmers say the loss of income is offset by the lower cost of growing.

Coffee is a labor-intensive crop. The beans must be handpicked, and then they go through several stages of processing. When the world market for coffee declines, coffee pickers are affected first. The uncertainty of the work sometimes causes a labor shortage as workers look for jobs with more security.

Many coffee farms around Boquete offer tours of their operations. After touring the farms, visitors head to the mill and then to a roasting facility. The tour ends with a "cupping," where visitors can taste the various blends of coffee grown on the farm.

Panamanian farmers also grow bananas, sugar, and rice. Some of the bananas and sugar are exported, but Panamanians are too fond of rice for there to be any left over to export.

Much of Panama does not have ideal farming conditions. Torrential rains pelt the Atlantic side during much of the year. Because of the rain, poor soil, and mountainous terrain, not many crops can be easily grown. Only the Pacific side has a predictable dry season from December to April, allowing farmers there to produce crops consistently. But even there farmers often don't practice conservation measures. The resulting erosion takes a toll on the already thin topsoil.

Panama's booming service industry is the backbone of its economy. A service industry is one that does not manufacture or grow anything but rather provides services such as banking and tourism.

Tourists and the people who cater to them love Panama for several reasons other than its incredible natural beauty. Panama has good roads, safe drinking water, and fine medical facilities. Panama City is as sophisticated as any American or European city. There are a great many international restaurants where foods of every country are served, and after dinner a visitor might walk along the Avenida Central to see the old part of town.

More adventurous tourists might travel to Portobelo and go ziplining through the rain forest between platforms that are perched in the trees high above the forest floor. While in Portobelo, a tourist might also want to go scuba diving in the Caribbean.

The Colón Free Trade Zone is another service industry. It is located near the Caribbean coastal city of Colón. A free trade zone is an area set aside where business can be transacted without being charged the usual taxes. Many countries maintain facilities in free trade zones for warehousing, repackaging, and re-exporting goods all over the world. The Colón Zone is the second largest free trade zone in the world and is one of the strengths of Panama's economy. The business it attracts is worth more than the money lost through tax breaks.

On market days, farmers bring their produce to town to sell in a central plaza or building. In Panama City the markets are open every day. If a fruit, vegetable, or grain is grown anywhere in Panama and is in season, you will find it for sale at Panama's main market.

The Panama Canal is the most visible of Panama's service industries. Panama's economy was hit hard when the U.S. military and their dependents withdrew from the Canal Zone in the late 1990s. In spite of Panama's desire to run its own country and canal, Panamanians missed the U.S. dollars in their pockets.

Since the Panamanians have taken control of canal operations, the number and the size of the container ships and cruise ships that use it have increased. The expansion that began in 2007 will keep the canal profitable for the foreseeable future.

Las Tablas on the Azuero Peninsula is a small town with a big reputation for the ultimate Carnival celebration. Townspeople choose two rival queens —one from Calle Arriba (high street) and one from Calle Abajo (low street). The queens and their courts compete to have the most elaborate costumes and flamboyant floats.

The Melting Pot

Panama is a richly diverse country full of people from many different backgrounds. Because of its long relationship with the United States and the number of laborers who moved to Panama to build the canal, the country has become a Latin American melting pot. While the culture is still distinctly Spanish, it has been influenced by Americans, Irish, Indians, Chinese, English, French, Germans, Malays, Jamaicans, and East Indians.

The extended family is the most important part of life in Panama. Taking care of one's family bows to all other obligations, and a Panamanian's home is reserved for family events. Almost all social and business entertaining is done at restaurants. If you receive an invitation to visit a Panamanian's home, you can be sure that you are highly regarded.

Panamanians love a good celebration, and that means lots of food. Food in Panama is not usually as spicy as in some Latin American countries. There also aren't as many green vegetables because they don't grow well in the tropical climate. A side dish that you might see on the table is fried plantains, which look like fat bananas but are used as vegetables. These versatile fruits can be cut crossways into disks, fried, pressed, and fried again. It's better to eat them when hot, because when they cool, they will turn to fruity concrete.

Panamanians also eat a lot of fish, shrimp, squid, and octopus. A favorite

Fried plantains

dish that you might find on the table at a family celebration is *sancocho,* a thick soup made with chicken, yucca, and a variety of vegetables. Or you might find the ever-popular arroz con pollo, which is chicken and rice.

Street vendors in the cities sell empanadas, which are flour or corn turnovers stuffed with spiced ground meat and fried. Tamales are also popular treats. Made from boiled ground corn and stuffed with chicken or pork and spices, tamales are then wrapped in banana leaves and boiled.

All of these foods and more are found at the numerous festivals that Panamanians attend. There's hardly a small village in Panama that doesn't have some kind of festival at least once a year. There, families eat, drink, dance, and have a good time.

The biggest festival is Carnival, which takes place right before the start of Lent, the forty days before Easter. Carnival in Panama is celebrated at the same time as Mardi Gras in New Orleans. It is a family affair, even though the alcohol flows freely. There are daily parades with festival queens and floats. Children shout and run after the floats and bands in the parades. The music is loud and fireworks pop on nearly every street.

A favorite part of the celebration is the Culecos, a street party that is basically a big water fight. Water trucks with hoses travel through the streets each morning of Carnival, spraying the lingering partygoers, who are by this time hot and tired after long hours of dancing. The water fight goes on even when there is a water shortage. Residents are just urged by officials to conserve water in the days before Carnival begins.

La Festival Nacional de La Mejorana is one of the more famous local festivals. It is held in Guararé on the Azuero Peninsula each September. It is a folkloric festival, which means that all of the music and dancing are in traditional Panamanian style. The festival draws hundreds of participants for the many dancing, singing, and instrument-playing contests that are offered. Organizers prohibit any kind of modern or foreign music or dance during the festival. They don't even allow a modern six-string guitar to be used.

At the Panama Jazz Festival, world-class jazz groups such as the Monk Institute Ensemble perform throughout Panama City. Panamanian pianist and educator Danilo Peréz started the festival in 2004 and has seen it grow from four concerts to fifteen, along with dozens of clinics, panels, and workshops.

A popular event for the Mejorana festival is La Atolladero, or day of the mud fight. Everyone comes out to sling mud at friends and family. The festival queen and her attendants dress in pure white so that the mud will show up better.

Music fans looking for a festival in January can attend the Panama Jazz Festival, held in Panama City. It features performances by and classes taught by world-famous jazz musicians.

Also happening in January is the Boquete Flower and Coffee Festival. This festival goes on for ten days and attracts visitors from all over Panama. The hotels in Boquete are booked months ahead of time.

Festivals are at the heart of Panama's culture. It's always a good day for a Panamanian family when they can attend a festival together. It will be the same for tourists when they visit and join in the fun.

In San José Church stands the famous Golden Altar, an elaborate baroque-style wooden altar that is plated in gold. The gold probably came from Peru during the early years of Spanish rule.

At Home in Panama

Children in Panama have to crawl out of bed on Monday morning and go to school just like most kids in North America. Public schools were started right after Panama gained its independence in 1903. Over 90 percent of the people in Panama can read, which is a high percentage among Latin American countries.

School attendance is required for children between the ages of six and fifteen years old. When finished with primary school, students can attend secondary schools to prepare for a job or college.

Religion is very important in Panama, where about 85 percent of the people are Catholic. Panama's religious roots go back to the Spanish conquest. Although Spain was most concerned with finding sources of gold, it also wanted to convert the Amerindians to Catholicism. The conquistadors left missions scattered across Latin America.

In the old part of Panama City is the Catedral de Nuestra Señora de la Asunción. This church took more than 100 years to build after construction began in 1688. It is located on the historic Plaza de la Independencia, where Panama declared its independence in 1903.

Also in the old section of Panama City is the Church of the Golden Altar. Legend says that the golden altar was saved from the infamous pirate Henry Morgan when he sacked Panama City in 1671. Supposedly a priest had the altar painted black, which hid its true value.

The small town of San Francisco in central Panama is home to a church called Iglesia San Francisco de la Montaña. It dates from 1727 and combines European and indigenous images and traditions. It has nine carved baroque altars, which are painted red and gold. There are also carvings that are distinctly non-Christian. The combination is unusual in Panama.

Panama is known for its religious freedom and tolerance. Besides Catholics, other religious groups there include Protestants, Muslims, and Jewish people. Some native tribes still practice a version of their traditional religions. Islam, the faith of the Muslims, is thought to have arrived in Latin America with Muslim African slaves in the 1500s.

Because religion plays such an important part in the everyday life of Panamanians, there are many holidays and events that center on religious observances. Many of the local festivals honor a town or village's patron saint.

On the national level, Panamanians flock to Portobelo for the Festival del Cristo Negro, the Festival of the Black Christ. They go to the Church of San Felipe, which is home to a life-sized wooden effigy of the Nazarene of Portobelo, or Black Christ.

There are several legends about the Black Christ, but most have to do with the statue saving Portobelo residents from shipwreck or cholera. The festival is a time to pray to the Black Christ for healing or to thank him for some good fortune. Pilgrims arrive in Portobelo from throughout Panama. Many come by foot, and some crawl on their hands and knees to show their devotion. Once they arrive, the pilgrims crowd into San Felipe to worship before the effigy.

After Mass is celebrated in the church and the statue is carried through the streets on a litter, it's time to celebrate in true Panamanian style. The pilgrims dance and drink the night away.

Holidays in Panama are taken seriously. Businesses close and nearly everyone celebrates. Most holidays are in honor of religious or patriotic events. After Carnival in the spring comes Labor Day on May 1, but by far the most holidays are celebrated in November.

November 3, 4, and 5 mark the holidays of Separation Day, Flag Day, and Colón Day. Separation Day marks the day that Panama separated from Colombia. Flag Day honors the flag, and Colón Day is Panama's version of Columbus Day.

The robes of the Black Christ statue are changed twice a year. The statue wears a wine-colored robe for October's Festival of the Black Christ. It wears a purple one for Holy Week, the week of Easter, in the spring. Many of the robes are donated anonymously.

November 10 observes the Uprising in the Villa de Los Santos, when the citizens of Los Santos declared their independence from Spain. This example spurred Panama City to act on behalf of the whole country. The countrywide declaration of independence from Spain came on November 28.

That leaves Mother's Day for December 8 and Christmas on December 25. A week later is New Year's Day, followed by Martyr's Day on January 9.

A Ngobe (NOH-bay) girl wears the colorful dress typical of all Ngobe women. Although the Ngobe and Bugle (BOO-glay) tribes speak different languages, they are culturally similar and are often spoken of as the Ngobe-Bugle. They live in the western mountains of Panama on a comarca.

Entertainment and Entertainers

Panamanians take a lot of family trips, whether it's a weekend trip to the beach or a week in Panama City to attend the theater or watch a soccer game. Families love to have fun, and there are plenty of places to do that in Panama.

With 1,547 miles (2,490 kilometers) of coastline, there are plenty of beaches for a day trip or a longer stay. The Bocas del Toro archipelago on the northern end of Panama offers outstanding beaches, some suitable for surfing. Sea turtles lay their eggs on the Bocas del Toro beaches. From March to June, huge leatherback sea turtles nest on beaches throughout the Bocas Islands. Local guides take tour groups to see the nesting turtles at night.

On the Pacific side of Panama beachgoers can visit the Pearl Islands. The most popular island in the Archipiélago de las Perlas is Contadora. Located 20 minutes by plane or two hours by boat from Panama City, Contadora has many white sand beaches, including the secluded Playa Cacique.

Farther south on the coast is Pinas Bay, which is the place to go for deep-sea fishing. The bay is located on the Pacific coast only 35 miles (56 kilometers) from Colombia. More deep-sea fishing world records have been set there than anywhere else in the world. Fishermen reel in black, blue, or striped marlin and Pacific sailfish.

If fishing doesn't sound interesting, a visitor can go to Playa Blanca (White Beach), located just north of Pinas Bay. Playa Blanca offers snorkeling in clear blue water near a coral reef just offshore.

Visitors enjoy snorkeling near the Punta Caracol Acqua Lodge, which is built right on the shallow water off Isla Colón in the Bocas del Toro archipelago. The lodge is connected to the island by a long wooden walkway.

Sports are just as popular in Panama as they are in the United States. Panama has produced several great boxers, including Roberto Duran. Duran held world titles in four different weight classes and won 104 of 120 career fights before retiring in 2002.

Horse racing in Panama has produced great jockeys, such as Hall-of-Fame member Laffit Pincay Jr. With 9,531 wins, Laffitt is the winningest jockey in history. He retired in 2003. Most of his racing was done in the United States.

Of course there is soccer, which is called football in Panama. Julio César Dely Valdés began his career in 1989 and is considered one of the best soccer players to come from Central America. Valdés has been a coach since 2006.

The largest number of successful professional athletes to come from Panama have played Major League Baseball in the United States. Rod Carew is a Hall-of-Fame first and second baseman who had 3,053 ca-

Rubén Blades

reer hits before retiring in 1986. New York Yankees pitcher Mariano Rivera is known for his dominance as a closer. Houston Astros' left fielder Carlos Lee is so tough, he's known as El Caballo (The Horse).

Music in Panama features salsa, cumbia, meringue, reggae, and Latin pop. At the National Theater in Panama City, you can experience a concert performed by the Panama Symphony Orchestra.

Rubén Blades is one of Panama's most famous musicians. Blades went to college and law school at the University of Panama. Shortly after he graduated

Carlos Lee

in 1972, and after his father tangled with Manuel Noriega, his family was sent into exile. Blades ended up in New York City where he changed his career plan from law to music.

Blades composed and sang salsa music, which is usually described as Cuban/Caribbean with Latin rhythms and styles. He earned a Grammy in 1987 for his album *Escenas* and had many other top-selling albums and songs. In the midst of his successful career as a musician, he began acting. Since 1983, he has appeared in more than 30 movies.

In another dramatic career change, Blades returned to Panama and ran for president in 1994. He came in third. Then, in 2004, he began yet another career when President Martín Torrijos appointed him Minister of Tourism. When his term ended in the summer of 2009, Blades returned to music.

The Miraflores Locks were built slightly inland from the Pacific Ocean to protect them from bombardment by enemy ships at sea. Air bombardment was not considered, since the Wright Brothers' 1903 flight at Kitty Hawk had barely taken place when canal planning began.

A visit to the Panama Canal is at the top of the list of almost every tourist who comes to this tropical country. After a hundred years it remains one of the most awe-inspiring feats of human construction. Plans to update the canal merely expand the wonder so that it can accommodate larger ships. The Interoceanic Canal Museum in Panama City is a great place to start a tour of Panama and the Panama Canal. The museum has many exhibits telling how the Panama Canal was built and operates.

It is possible to travel by boat through the canal and its locks (you don't have to be on a tanker to go through), and there are many other sights to see along the way and at each end. Panama Canal transits are offered on Saturdays—full transits take most of a day, but some people choose to go only partway across, which takes 4 to 5 hours. Most tourists take the trip as part of a package deal offered by tour companies.

The canal locks are the main attraction on the canal. The Miraflores Locks, which link the Pacific Ocean to Miraflores Lake, raise and lower ships 54 feet (16.5 meters) in two steps. Near the Miraflores Locks, the Miraflores Visitors Center contains an observation deck plus a four-story museum about the canal and its history. One floor of the museum has a full-scale pilot training simulator and a topographical map of the canal.

The next locks are a short distance up the canal at Pedro Miguel. This one-step lock raises and lowers ships 31 feet (9.5 meters) from

The Panama Canal has been called the greatest engineering feat of the twentieth century, with its massive locks along 50 miles (80 km) of canal. But how does it work? Why aren't there pumps to fill the locks? Why doesn't Gatun Lake run out of water? And why couldn't the French build their big ditch straight through from Colón to Panama City?

The French had successfully built the Suez Canal in Egypt in the 1860s, and the designer of that canal, Ferdinand De Lesseps, was sure he could do the same in Panama in the 1880s. As brilliant as De Lesseps was, he didn't take into account one important factor—the Suez Canal was built at sea level from one end to the other. Panama's interior had mountains, not the level sand of Egypt.

To build a sea-level canal in Panama, the French would have to dig through thousands of feet of mountains and jungles. The canal bottom would have to be relatively flat for the water to flow from one side to the other. Their plan didn't work.

When U.S. engineers began planning the Panama Canal, they knew they would need to use a system of locks. Locks are like steps that take a ship up or down to the next level of water. With locks, water can be moved above the land.

Locks are built of cement and look like huge swimming pools. They have a fairly simple design to raise and lower the water levels in

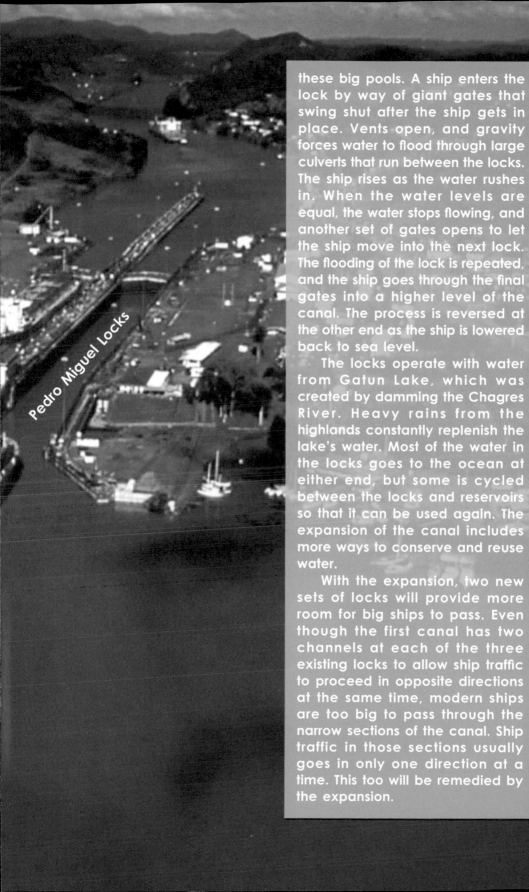

Pedro Miguel Locks

these big pools. A ship enters the lock by way of giant gates that swing shut after the ship gets in place. Vents open, and gravity forces water to flood through large culverts that run between the locks. The ship rises as the water rushes in. When the water levels are equal, the water stops flowing, and another set of gates opens to let the ship move into the next lock. The flooding of the lock is repeated, and the ship goes through the final gates into a higher level of the canal. The process is reversed at the other end as the ship is lowered back to sea level.

The locks operate with water from Gatun Lake, which was created by damming the Chagres River. Heavy rains from the highlands constantly replenish the lake's water. Most of the water in the locks goes to the ocean at either end, but some is cycled between the locks and reservoirs so that it can be used again. The expansion of the canal includes more ways to conserve and reuse water.

With the expansion, two new sets of locks will provide more room for big ships to pass. Even though the first canal has two channels at each of the three existing locks to allow ship traffic to proceed in opposite directions at the same time, modern ships are too big to pass through the narrow sections of the canal. Ship traffic in those sections usually goes in only one direction at a time. This too will be remedied by the expansion.

Miraflores Lake to the Gaillard Cut. Originally called the Culebra Cut, this huge slash through the mountains of the Continental Divide provides a channel for the canal. It was renamed the Gaillard Cut after Major David Gaillard, the engineer in charge of the cut.

The Gaillard Cut was the most difficult section of the Panama Canal to construct because of the almost constant cave-ins of the freshly dug ditches. Every method old and new was used to stop the collapses, but nothing worked. The geological makeup of the cut was so complex that some thought the canal would never be finished. Major Gaillard gave up in despair and went home to the United States. The workers and machines dug on until the ditch was finally wide enough to stabilize, with only occasional landslides to slow canal traffic.

Midway on the canal is Gamboa, a small city famous for its outstanding natural beauty. It is the gateway to Parque Nacional Soberanía, one of Panama's many national parks. This park runs on the east side of the canal from Gamboa to Lake Gatun near the town of Limón. It is one of the most accessible tropical forests in the world.

Lake Gatun was formed after the Chagres River was dammed to provide more water for the Panama Canal. When the project was finished, Gatun became the largest artificial lake in the world. When ships cross the lake, they still follow the submerged original channel of the Chagres River.

The Gatun Locks raise and lower ships 85 feet in three steps on the Caribbean side of Panama. The three pairs of locks make a massive display, as they extend almost a mile.

A canal expansion project is under way to add two new sets of locks, deepen the Gaillard Cut, and make other changes and improvements to the existing canal. The projected completion date is 2014. The expansion will allow the canal to accommodate post-Panamax ships—ships that are too big to fit through the original canal.

Upon exiting the canal in the Caribbean, ships come upon the islands of Kuna Yala. This archipelago of nearly 400 islands is part of the Comarca de Kuna Yala, which also includes a strip of mountainous forested land on the mainland of Panama.

Capuchin monkeys in the Gamboa Reservation in Panama. These monkeys can be found in Central and South America, and as far south as northern Argentina. Capuchins are believed to be the most intelligent New World monkeys.

An estimated 40,000 of the indigenous Kuna people live on about 40 of these small islands rather than on the mainland. The other islands are uninhabited but open to tourists. These tropical islands are complete with palm trees, warm sand, and blue water. Swimming, snorkeling, and hammock swinging are the usual entertainments there.

The Kuna have maintained their native culture to a much larger degree than many other Central American indigenous peoples. Kuna women dress traditionally in colorful skirts and blouses. The blouses are decorated with complicated panels called *molas*. The panels are done in a type of reverse appliqué technique that uses many layers of brightly colored cloth to reveal intricate designs. Kuna women make and sell *molas,* which have become collectors' items throughout the world. The sale of *molas* and other crafts supplement the Kuna income, which otherwise comes from fishing and other island occupations.

Back across the isthmus from Kuna Yala is Panama City. It is considered the most sophisticated of all Central American cities. International business is one of the main reasons for its vibrant personality. A visitor can find almost any kind of entertainment, food, or lodging there.

Panama is more than just the home of the Panama Canal, but there is little doubt that the building of the canal shaped the modern nation. The monumental construction project left more behind when the cranes and excavators departed than just a big ditch. Left behind were technological advances, up-to-date health care, and far fewer mosquitoes.

Kuna woman holding a *mola*

Even more important, the canal project left behind a national pride of accomplishment that helped Panama through many years of political upheaval. Today Panama has clean water, good roads, a modern infrastructure, and a growing economy. Panama is a Latin American example of success.

A tourist would be hard pressed to travel anywhere in Panama and not see something interesting and even astonishing. From the beauty of its beaches and rain forest to the sophistication of its cities, Panama offers the traveler both adventure and relaxation. It has even become popular as a retirement destination for Americans and Europeans. They may come to visit but return to live permanently in what they consider a tropical paradise.

Mola

The Kuna Indians of Panama are world famous for their reverse appliqué *molas* made of brightly colored cotton fabrics. The word *mola* means "blouse" in their language, and the *mola* panels are usually sewn on women's blouses. Some *molas* are also placed on tote bags or used as wall hangings. With some paper, paste, and scissors, it's possible to make a paper design just like those of the Kunas.

Supplies
9" x 12" construction paper or card stock (black, white, and other colors)
Scissors
Glue stick or paste

Directions
1. Draw a simple outline of a bird, bug, or flower on one of the sheets of colored paper. Cut it out.
2. Glue the shape onto a sheet of different colored paper. Enlarge the design by cutting around the shape, leaving about ¼ inch of the background paper showing.
3. Repeat on a different colored paper.
4. Continue to enlarge the shape this way, using colored or white paper.
5. When the design is as large as you want, glue it onto a sheet of black paper.
6. Cut cigar-shaped pieces of various lengths from paper scraps. Glue them on the shape and on the black paper surrounding your shape.

Tips
Card stock paper makes the brightest *molas*.
You can use different colors of felt to make a soft *mola*.
For smoother lines, move the paper rather than the scissors when cutting, and be sure your scissors are sharp.

Tortillas

Panamanian tortillas are made of corn flour and are not flat like Mexican tortillas. They are thicker and puff up even more when cooked. Panamanians eat tortillas like Americans might eat biscuits or some other kind of bread. This recipe makes five to seven tortillas, depending on how big you make them.

Ingredients
2 cups masa (corn tortilla mix)
½ cup grated farmers cheese (a soft white cheese)
½ teaspoon salt
1 cup water
Vegetable oil
Cheddar or other cheese for melting on top

In a medium bowl, mix the masa with the grated farmers cheese and salt. Gradually add the water as you stir. The dough should be soft and a little sticky. Use a little more water if the dough doesn't stick together. Mix the dough with your hands until you can form small balls about the size of golf balls. Flatten each dough ball with your hands, smoothing the edges, until the disk is about ¼ inch thick.

Under **adult supervision**, cover the bottom of a skillet with oil and heat to medium high. There should be just enough oil for the bottom edges of the tortillas to sizzle when first placed in the pan. Place the dough circles in the hot oil. You can cook as many at a time as you have room for in your skillet, but it is easier to cook the tortillas one or two at a time. Fry the tortillas about 6 to 8 minutes, turning them frequently to prevent scorching. If they brown too quickly, reduce the heat slightly. They will be golden brown when done and have some darker brown marks. Remove from the skillet and place on a plate lined with paper towels to drain.

Top with cheddar or other cheese while hot. Panamanians often eat tortillas for breakfast with eggs and many kinds of toppings. You can try salsa, beans, ground beef, green onions, or just about any other kind of topping.

For a more American taste, skip the melted cheese and top with grape jelly. When the tortillas cool a bit, you can even try peanut butter and jelly topping.

BCE

9000	Earliest evidence of humans in Panama.
5000	People begin to farm on the Pacific coast of central Panama.
2500	Decorated ceramics appear—they are the oldest in Central America.

CE

750–950	Cemetery at Sitio Conte in use. Site of rich find of pre-Columbian artifacts.
800–1100	In Parque Arqueológico del Caño near Sitio Conte, huge stone columns shaped as animals and humans mark off a ceremonial ground or playing field.
1501	Spanish explorer Rodrigo de Bastidas sails along the Caribbean coast of Panama.
1502	Christopher Columbus explores Panama's Caribbean coast.
1513	After crossing Panama, Vasco Núñez de Balboa first sees the Pacific Ocean.
1519	Panama City is founded.
1698	Scottish settlers found colony of New Edinburgh in the Darién Scheme. The colony is abandoned by 1700.
1821	Panama declares independence from Spain and joins Gran Colombia, an alliance between Colombia, Venezuela, and Ecuador.
1848–50	California gold rush brings forty-niners by the thousands to Panama; they want to cross the isthmus and reach California quickly.
1855	Panama Railroad is completed.
1881	Under Ferdinand De Lesseps, France begins digging a canal across the isthmus.
1888	De Lesseps's Panama Canal Company goes bankrupt.
1903	Panama declares independence from Colombia. The Hay-Bunau-Varilla Treaty is signed, giving the United States the right to build the Panama Canal.
1904	The U.S. begins building the Panama Canal.
1914	The Panama Canal opens.
1925	Kuna Indians of the San Blas Islands, led by Nene Kantule, declare independence from the rest of Panama.
1947	Treaty that allows the United States to continue to use military bases outside the Canal Zone is rejected after protesters riot.
1964	After an agreement to fly both the Panamanian flag and the U.S. flag within the Canal Zone, students at an American high school fly the U.S. flag by itself, sparking the Panama Canal Riots.
1968	Panama's National Guard Lieutenant Colonel Omar Torrijos and Major Boris Martínez lead a successful military coup to depose President Arnulfo Arias.
1972	Torrijos introduces a new constitution. The Kuna Indians gain elected representation in the General Assembly.
1977	Torrijos and U.S. President Jimmy Carter sign treaties to gradually return control of the Panama Canal to Panama.
1981	Torrijos is killed in a plane crash.
1983	General Manuel Noriega is firmly in control of Panama.
1985	Noriega opponent Dr. Hugo Spadafora is tortured and beheaded. Noriega is implicated in the murder.
1989	Election held in May; Noriega voids results. In December, Operation Just Cause begins. Guillermo Endara is sworn in as president. Noriega surrenders to U.S.
1990	Panamanian military is disbanded.
1999	First woman president of Panama, Mireya Moscoso, takes office. Control of the canal is turned over to Panama.
2006	The third Panama Canal locks project is approved by national referendum.
2007	Work on the new locks begins.
2009	President Ricardo Martinelli is elected.
2010	Manuel Noriega is extradited to France to face money-laundering charges.

Books

Augustin, Byron. *Panama.* New York: Children's Press, 2005.

Mann, Elizabeth. *The Panama Canal: The Story of How a Jungle Was Conquered and the World Made Smaller.* New York: Mikaya Press, 2006.

Petrie, Kristin. *Vasco Núñez de Balboa.* Edina, MN: Checkerboard Books, 2007.

Roberts, Russell. *Building the Panama Canal.* Hockessin, DE: Mitchell Lane Publishers, 2008.

Shields, Charles. *Panama.* Broomall, PA: Mason Crest Publishers, 2008.

Works Consulted

Crowther, Heloise. *Culture Smart! Panama.* London: Kuperard, 2006.

Friar, William. *Moon Panama.* Berkeley, CA: Avalon Travel, 2008.

Greene, Julie. *The Canal Builders.* New York: The Penguin Press, 2009.

Harding, Robert. *The History of Panama.* Westport, CT: Greenwood Press, 2006.

Howarth, David. *Panama: Four Hundred Years of Dreams and Cruelty.* New York, 1966.

Libert, Lucien. "Panama's Ex-dictator Noriega 'Very Weak': Lawyer." Reuters, April 29, 2010. http://www.reuters.com/article/idUSTRE63S3M520100429

McCullough, David. *The Path Between the Seas.* New York: Simon and Schuster, 1977.

McMillan, Robert. *Global Passage: Transformation of Panama and the Panama Canal.* Charleston, SC: Booksurge, 2006.

Mitchinson, Martin. *The Darién Gap.* Madeira Park, British Colombia: Harbour Publishing Co., Ltd, 2008.

Parker, Matthew. *Panama Fever.* New York: Doubleday, 2007.

St. Louis, Regis, and Scott Doggett. *Panama.* Oakland, CA: Lonely Planet Publications, 2004.

On the Internet

Canal Museum
    http://canalmuseum.com
CIA—The World Factbook—Panama
    https://www.cia.gov/library/publications/the-world-factbook/geos/pm.html
Interoceanic Canal Museum (in Spanish)
    http://www.museodelcanal.com/
Panama Canal Authority
    http://www.pancanal.com
The Panama News: Panama's Online English-Language Newspaper
    http://thepanamanews.com
The Panama Railroad
    http://www.panamarailroad.org/
U.S. Department of State: Diplomacy in Action; "Panama"
    http://www.state.gov/r/pa/ei/bgn/2030.htm

appliqué (ap-lih-KAY)—A decoration or trimming of one material that is sewn or glued (applied) to another material.

archipelago (ar-kih-PEH-luh-goh)—A group or chain of islands.

biodiversity (by-oh-dih-VER-sih-tee)—The variety of living things in a particular area or region.

cholera (KAH-luh-ruh)—An acute intestinal infection caused by eating or drinking food or water contaminated with the *Vibrio cholerae* bacterium. It can quickly lead to severe dehydration and death if not treated promptly.

coup (KOO)—The sudden forcible overthrow of a government, usually by its own army.

effigy (EF-ih-jee)—A statue or likeness of a person.

extradition (ex-truh-DIH-shun)—The turning over of a person accused of a crime to another country, state, or county for prosecution of a crime that was allegedly committed in that jurisdiction.

fumigate (FYOO-mih-gayt)—Spreading vapors or fumes to disinfect or rid an area of unwanted insects or other pests.

indigenous (in-DIH-juh-nuhs)—Living or growing naturally in a region or country.

isthmus (IS-mus)—A narrow strip of land that connects two larger bodies of land and has water on each side.

malaria (mah-LAYR-ee-uh)—A deadly disease that is transmitted by certain kinds of mosquitoes.

oligarchy (OH-lih-gar-kee)—A form of government in which the ruling power belongs to a few people or families.

perpetuity (per-peh-TOO-ih-tee)—An unlimited time period.

quarantine (KWAR-un-teen)—To isolate a person with a contagious disease in order to stop the spread of that disease.

renovation (reh-noh-VAY-shun)—To repair or redo so as to make something like new.

topography (tah-PAH-gruh-fee)—The shape of the land, including features such as mountains, rivers, and lakes.

Vatican (VAT-ih-kin)—The seat of the Catholic Church, located in Rome, Italy.

Bonnie Hinman is the author of 20 books for young people, including *We Visit Peru* and *The Massachusetts Bay Colony* for Mitchell Lane Publishers. Her biography of W.E.B. Du Bois, *A Stranger in My Own House*, published by Morgan Reynolds, was selected for inclusion on the 2006 New York Public Library list, Books for the Teen Age. She loves to read about other countries and was excited to finally learn how the Panama Canal operates. Hinman graduated from Missouri State University and lives in southwest Missouri with her husband, Bill. Her children and four grandchildren live nearby.